STONEHENGE

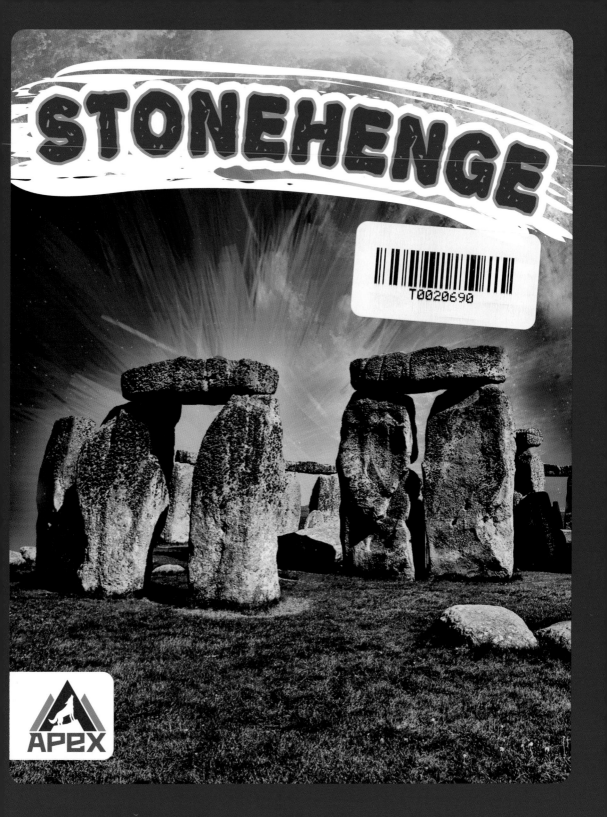

BY MEG GAERTNER

WWW.APEXEDITIONS.COM

Apex is distributed by North Star Editions:
sales@northstareditions.com | 888-417-0195

Produced for Apex by Red Line Editorial.

Photographs ©: Shutterstock Images, cover, 1, 4–5, 6–7, 8, 9, 10–11, 14, 15, 16–17, 20–21, 22–23, 24–25, 26–27, 29; iStockphoto, 12–13, 18, 19

Library of Congress Control Number: 2021915704

ISBN
978-1-63738-165-6 (hardcover)
978-1-63738-201-1 (paperback)
978-1-63738-270-7 (ebook pdf)
978-1-63738-237-0 (hosted ebook)

Printed in the United States of America
Mankato, MN
012022

NOTE TO PARENTS AND EDUCATORS

Apex books are designed to build literacy skills in striving readers. Exciting, high-interest content attracts and holds readers' attention. The text is carefully leveled to allow students to achieve success quickly. Additional features, such as bolded glossary words for difficult terms, help build comprehension.

TABLE OF CONTENTS

CHAPTER 1

MIDWINTER DAY

It is the **winter solstice**. The day is short and cold. The sun shines on a circle of huge stones.

Stonehenge had 30 stones standing tall in a circle. These stones held up other slabs that lay flat.

A trilithon has two stones standing tall and a flat stone across the top.

Inside the circle, bigger stones form a **horseshoe**. People gather near them. The people watch the sun set between the two tallest stones.

The horseshoe includes 15 stones. Some are 23 feet (7 m) tall.

Night comes quickly. It is the longest night of the year. But the people feast. From now on, days will start getting longer again.

Some stories say strange things happen at Stonehenge after dark.

As the seasons change, the sun rises and sets between different stones in the circle.

CHANGING SEASONS

When Stonehenge was built, many people farmed. Seasons were important to them. Many crops grow in spring and summer. People gather food in the fall. In the winter, not much grows.

CHAPTER 2

BUILDING STONEHENGE

Stonehenge is a large stone **monument** in England. The circle of stones is 100 feet (30 m) across. It's surrounded by open fields.

A much wider circle of earth surrounds the stone circle. It is about 330 feet (101 m) across.

Some bluestones used at Stonehenge came all the way from Wales. They had to be moved more than 100 miles (161 km).

Building Stonehenge would have been difficult. Its huge vertical stones came from 20 miles (32 km) away. Smaller stones were moved even farther.

Some of the vertical stones weigh more than 25 tons (23 metric tons).

Builders also shaped the stones. They dug holes in the ground. Then they pulled the stones into place.

England has several other rings of standing stones. For example, Avebury has the biggest stone circle in the world.

When Stonehenge was made, builders didn't use wheels or metal tools.

People may have scraped smaller rocks along the stones to smooth them.

A LONG BUILD

Stonehenge was built in many stages. About 5,000 years ago, it was just a circular ditch. The huge stones were added over hundreds of years.

CHAPTER 3

THE LEGENDS

People today are not sure why Stonehenge was built. Many theories have been suggested. Some ideas are less likely than others.

Some people claim that aliens helped build Stonehenge.

In the 1100s, one writer said a **wizard** built Stonehenge. The wizard's name was Merlin. He used magic to lift the stones. People believed this story into the 1500s.

The wizard Merlin (left) often gave people help and advice. One story says he built Stonehenge to remember people who had died there.

King Arthur's Knights of the Round Table were named for the place where they sat to make plans.

KING ARTHUR

Merlin appears in the **legend** of King Arthur. Arthur became king by pulling a sword from a stone. He led a group of knights. They fought to protect the people of Britain.

Later, people believed the **Druids** built Stonehenge. The stone circle was their main temple. But it was built thousands of years before the Druids came to the area.

Some Druids still gather at Stonehenge for festivals.

CHAPTER 4

THE EVIDENCE

Scientists study Stonehenge. They've found **evidence** for some theories. Stonehenge likely had many uses over the years.

Stonehenge may have been used for burials, religious events, or keeping track of time.

Human bones and ashes have been found at Stonehenge. Many scientists agree it was once a burial ground. People brought their dead to Stonehenge.

A PLACE OF HEALING

The smaller stones at Stonehenge are bluestones. Legends say they can heal. Builders may have brought them to Stonehenge for this reason. Sick people might have gone to Stonehenge to get well.

Stacks of stones called dolmens are found throughout Europe. Researchers think they were used for burials.

Stonehenge's stones were placed very carefully. They lined up with the sun's movements. They likely helped people track the changing seasons.

During the summer solstice, the sun rose between two stones.

A stone outside the circle marks the spot where the sun will rise on the summer solstice.

COMPREHENSION QUESTIONS

Write your answers on a separate piece of paper.

1. Write a sentence summarizing the main ideas of Chapter 2.

2. Would you want to see Stonehenge in real life? Why or why not?

3. Which theory about why Stonehenge was built does the most evidence support?

> **A.** The wizard Merlin used magic to build Stonehenge.
> **B.** Farmers built Stonehenge to mark the changing seasons.
> **C.** The Druids built Stonehenge to be their temple.

4. Why would it have been hard to move the vertical stones long distances?

> **A.** The stones were very big and heavy.
> **B.** The land near Stonehenge is full of trees.
> **C.** The builders could only use metal tools.

5. What does **theories** mean in this book?

*People today are not sure why Stonehenge was built. Many **theories** have been suggested. Some ideas are less likely than others.*

    A. suggestions for how to do something
    B. ideas meant to explain something
    C. people who build something

6. What does **burial** mean in this book?

*Many scientists agree it was once a **burial** ground. People brought their dead to Stonehenge.*

    A. used for burying the dead
    B. used to heal people
    C. used to grow food

Answer key on page 32.

GLOSSARY

Druids
Religious leaders for the ancient Celts, who spread from mainland Europe to Britain and Ireland.

evidence
Facts or information that help prove a theory is true.

festivals
Days or times of celebration, often based on a religion.

horseshoe
Something in the shape of the letter U.

legend
A famous story, often based on facts but not always completely true.

monument
A structure or place that is important in history.

summer solstice
The day each year when one of Earth's poles is tilted closest to the sun. It is the longest day of the year.

winter solstice
The day each year when one of Earth's poles is tilted farthest from the sun. It is the shortest day of the year.

wizard
A person with magical powers, especially in fairy tales and legends.

TO LEARN MORE

BOOKS

Abdo, Kenny. *Lost Lands*. Minneapolis: Abdo Publishing, 2020.

Loh-Hagan, Virginia. *Stonehenge*. Ann Arbor, MI: Cherry Lake Publishing, 2018.

Weitzman, Elizabeth. *Mysteries of Stonehenge*. Minneapolis: Lerner Publications, 2018.

ONLINE RESOURCES

Visit **www.apexeditions.com** to find links and resources related to this title.

ABOUT THE AUTHOR

Meg Gaertner is a children's book editor and writer. She lives in Minneapolis, where she enjoys swing dancing and spending time outside.

INDEX

Answer Key:
1. Answers will vary; **2.** Answers will vary; **3.** B; **4.** A; **5.** B; **6.** A